You Are Your Thoughts Become Your Faith

By

Bernard Benson Sarfo

Also by Bernard Benson Sarfo

The Fact Among Facts (1st)
The Fact Among Facts

Standalone
The Youth Murderer
Be Original Not a Copy
The Christians Science or Scholarship
Precious than Paradise
Habit Makes Future
A shelter from storm and rain
The Science of Life
The Strongest Lion Knockback
The Perfect and Inspiring City
Above Hope, Faith and Love
The Hero's Brave Decisions
The Weakest Among Plants
The Hero's Brave Decisions
Doing Above The Ability
The Wisdom Beyond Power And Greatness

Heavier Than the Heavens
The Academics Brains and Recreation Logics
The Strange Voice
The Chaotic World
Don't Miss Your Flight
Let the Nations Ponder
You Are Your Thoughts

Table of Contents

Dedication

I dedicate this book to everyone in the world today.

'When wisdom entered into your heart, and knowledge is pleasant unto your soul, discretion shall preserve you, understanding shall keep you' (Proverbs 2:10, 11).

Introduction

In the beginning, God created the heavens and the earth, and the earth was formless and void.

The earth was formless and void defines the nature at the beginning of creation. Here defines the limit state of the earth at the beginning.

The earth was formless defines the incomplete state at the creation. The state, the beauty and the identity were absent and there was no character that defines the earth at the beginning.

What do I mean concerning these comments? In fact, you cannot identify anything without behavior and position.

The earth was at no condition to describe from its formation for the first time of creation. God created the man in his image and likeness, the man has the position and identity corresponding to his creator that makes his character. Here the man has the position and identity.

But the earth was formless or without character at the beginning of creation. But God prepares it by his word and fill the vacuums with objects to make it meaningful.

Our life on this earth must be meaningful and reasonable as God prepared earth at the beginning of creation.

Our character portraits the condition of our being and defines the meaning of our state. Every act or behaviour makes one's life meaningful or void, and there is no likeness without performances.

The trees have identities, birds have identities, and rivers have identities and so on. But without presentations, there is no uniqueness. Anyone who disregards God supervision lost his or her identity.

What do I mean? Or what concerns this book? I want you to know the condition or state of a life without God supervision, and the fruit that bears. Life without God guidance becomes formless and void like the state of this earth at the beginning. This world has full of darknesses and the condition without definition.

The earth has the history of its beginnings and the future which will define the results. Why God created this earth? What is his main purpose? Who did He create for? What does God expect from a man? How must we live?

What is our duty and what will be our reward? The earth was created purposely for man and it was designed to glorify God. The man was the manager to care, to dress and to keep it.

The whole heaven put their confidence or trust in the man to make this earth a sustainable and dwelling place for eternity. But the man could not make it as proposed by God.

We must keep in mind that we are here for a purpose or reason. We are created to make a difference and to maintain the beauty of this nature and to make here the second heaven but what emerges?

Note; this book is to remind us to remember our creator and to live like Him on this earth, not by might or power but by His Spirit.

As Christian, this must be our note and to keep in mind that we are in the presence of God each day, hour and night.

So, we must respect Him each moment and live for Him each time. God toke Enoch because he walked with Him.

Contents Pages

1. Thinking

Human beings are identifying by the way we act or think and move. Thinking makes us normal beings and differentiates us from other creatures. Without thinking there can be no movement and performance.

So, thinking identifies our movement and our effort. In every movement shows the thought and the action. Our characters and behaviour are the keys which open the doors of identities.

Our identifications show the kind of thinking and prove performance or action. The body acts and behaviour reviews the kind or type of thought at that moment.

The whole key of life whether the life will be better or not, whether life will lose eternity or not it depends on the type or the kind of thinking.

So, our life development and achievement stands on the way we think or judging. Our will and choice determine our thought. Thinking makes the difference between life and the attitude of every person.

It makes the difference in behavior and choice. Your value stands on your thinking and devalues also stands on your thought or judging. The difference between the wise and the foolish son show by their thought or act

Our abilities and doings result in the way we think. So, thinking or thought hold the whole life keys and shows the direction of the one heading towards. When the thoughts are good, the behaviour sounds well.

The same as the bad thoughts make the dullness of the being. Many have lost their identity because of bad thought and other has lost their chance because of indefinite thought.

Concerning our being as humans, make different from other creatures because God created us as His image and likeness.

As human beings, we have lost the real image of God and His likeness. That means we have lost the original identity of our being and the position as human beings.

But God intends to restore the lost identity to the original one. So, any kind of behaviour that is contrary to the original is not part of our being. Means any kind of activities contrary to the law of God is not of God.

Here, I want you to know that if you have any kind of behaviour contrary to the law of God, then you must watch out and allow God to change it for you. Else you will lose eternal life if it continues in the same way you see it.

Here thinking determines our state and identity. Everyone on this earth is going to account for his or her doings, and this is the act of thought that determines our direction.

So, anyone who acts opposing to the law of God is not of the family of heaven at the moment that acts occur. Our whole life and eternal destiny stand on the way we think and act.

As human beings, we need to be careful or watch out concerning our thought been review. If anything needs protection and guide even than our eyes and the whole being is our thought; because the whole life and destiny solution is decided by the brain.

This is true and there is no doubt about it. Our understanding which is the key master of our destiny that brings an answer to every situation makes the thought direction.

Here if the understanding fails then the whole life lost the right direction and then deviate. Everyone on this earth needs to understand that, the deviation of life is the act of thought or understanding.

We have so many incidences that everyone has the way he or she understands things and then explain.

Sin has damaged the correct understanding of human beings, and this has caused a big difference concerning the way we judge things. In this case, we need to know that, it is difficult for us to be saved because the whole nature has been subjected to errors.

Furthermore, the only way for us to be saved is to subject the whole being for God controlling. Else we cannot have the mind or thoughts of God or His image and likeness.

The original character needs to be restored and protected by God. Without this, we cannot be accepted.

Moreover, our identity which shows our position as sons of God reveals the character of God. And this shows the kind of thought we have and the direction we are heading towards.

Every son of God thinks and acts as His image and likeness. This identification portrait the kind of thought we have and give us a position as the sons and daughters of God.

Our thought is the whole life of our being and there is no identification without thought or performance. As human beings, whatever acts we reveal show the one who is leading us, whether good or bad makes us position and identity.

My brethren, we must be careful and be aware that this life has already had the decision because of the sin of our first parents, and there is nothing that we can do to change our condition.

Except we allow Christ to take possession of the heart. Apart from this, there is no other way for us to have the image and the likeness of God.

You need to ask yourself and answer for yourself concerning your thought as in the right direction? Any kind of thought makes life and death at each moment it comes.

So to our identity also revealed our state and position or direction we are coming from.

Whatever may be, you must identify yourself well or decide your position through the act of your understanding and then makes the difference between good and evil.

2. Talking

Talking is the first identification of a man, and it is a trade character for communication. Man cannot be a man without communication skills and the whole nature of a man is identifying by his speech.

In order to know someone well depends on his or her speech, whether the person is good or not stands on the tone voice out. Our speech makes us a whole as human beings and also demonstrates our ability.

The whole human trade in the world and the knowledge that man has depends on speech. Without communication, there is no existence, and without speech, there is no life.

In fact, human beings are known for their speech. So, speech is the identity of a person and the character of his or her being.

There are many languages in the world and these languages are the characters of each tribe. Their knowledge, their acts, the skills, culture and their progress depend on their language.

It is their key that opens their understanding. In fact, our development and acts depend on the language we understand. Life improvement stands on the understanding of the language used.

Here people can be confusing when the language used is out of their understanding. That is, it can stop their progress and destroy their ability as people or nation. Our life progress both physical and spiritual depends on the tongue we voice out.

Why all these comments? In fact, talking has a lot of influence in our lives and there is no way to prevent these influences. When we talk, we reveal our socialization and sometimes love towards our colleagues.

Socialization open ways for opportunities but good speech redecorate the character and makes progress. As human beings, we need to be more careful when talking to our neighbours.

Our speeches need to be mix with salt, and then to know how to welcome people. So, what will be the result of bad speech? Bad speech prevents people from approaching to you and also disgraces your ability.

Too much talking damages your glory and reduces your admiration. Our good acts and abilities sometimes destroy by unnecessary talk. The title of this book (Think as you are in Paradise) means we must live and talk as a heaven representative.

We need to know and understand that, every talking brings a curse or blessing to the listener and the one who is talking.

Wars and other misunderstanding most of them come by bad talks or communications. As Christians and God children, we need to train ourselves for good and best conversation.

We must keep mind that whatever speech or talk we voice out has a curse and blessing. We need to bless through our speech and encourage people when we are communicating with them.

The world cannot survive without communication but death is better than bad speech. So, when you speak wrong words you kill the soul and even damage your home. Good talking revives the soul and opens the ways for progress.

But bad or evil talk blocked the way for progress and also do away the glory and chance. If anything has power or influence that destroys the world faster than anything it is a bad speech or wrong communication.

The whole sources of blessing and the whole source of curse comes by talking. More can be done through talking and more can destroy through speech. In James chapter 3 makes it clear the result of the tongue and its penalties.

Let's read: Not many of you should become teachers, my brothers; for you know that we who teach will be judged with greater strictness.

For we all stumble in many ways. And if anyone does not stumble in what he says, he is a perfect man, able also to bridle his whole body.

If we put bits into the mouths of horses so that they obey us, we guide their whole bodies as well. Look at the ships also: though they are so large and are driven by strong winds, they are guided by a very small rudder wherever the will of the pilot directs.

So also the tongue is a small member, yet it boasts of great things. How great a forest is set ablaze by such a small fire! And the tongue is a fire, a world of unrighteousness.

The tongue is set among our members, staining the whole body, setting on fire the entire course of life, and set on fire by hell.

For every kind of beast and bird, of reptile and sea creature, can be tamed and has been tamed by mankind, but no human being can tame the tongue.

It is a restless evil, full of deadly poison. With it we bless our Lord and Father, and with it we curse people who are made in the likeness of God. From the same mouth come blessing and cursing.

My brothers, these things ought not to be so. Does a spring pour forth from the same opening both fresh and saltwater? Can a fig tree, my brothers, bear olives, or a grapevine produce figs?

Neither can a salt pond yield fresh water. If we look at what the Bible is saying, then there is great damage and poison in bad speech.

The person cannot identify well without his or her talk. So, we all need to be extra careful by our speech.

In all, everyone in this world must speak in a polite way and take care of each line of his or her speech.

As Christians, this should be our note and concern that our words must be profitable and blessing to all who hear us.

3. Eating

The most dangerous and benefit of our life is eating. Eating is not bad but bad eating is taking away the whole seawater. Means bad eating destroys the soul, the spirit and the body.

If there is anything good and best for a man to survive is eating. But every food that goes to the body must be simple, best and clean. Sufficient food must be taken on each day, and it is best to take twice per day than to take trice per day.

This is the preferred suggestion but not by any law or legal principle. The idea and the benefit behind taking food twice per day is best than the trice per day is that; first, it prolongs your structure beauty.

Secondly, it's maintaining your strength day in and day out. Thirdly, it prolongs your life and fourthly, it keeps you from getting disease habitually and then makes you sound and energetic always. What will be the effect of too much of eating or wrong habit of eating?

Our physical growth stands on eating but the strength of our spiritual matters stands on good, sufficient and the clean habit of eating. Our knowledge and ability stand on the habit of good eating and well balanced diet.

Too much of eating damage the soul and destroys good and best thought. In fact, spiritual matters are measured by the habit of good, sufficient, modest and clean habit of eating.

Men cannot be well measured concerning his spiritual matters by lacking the correct habit of eating. That is eating without measure or overdose.

The dullness of mind and the lack of good judgment cause by a bad habit of eating. Our knowledge, wisdom and understanding can be lost by a bad habit of eating. Every man cannot think well when taking too much of food.

Our system as human beings needs food that will maintain the structure for daily activity. We are not created to be food conscious beings, but as reasonable and responsible beings in all matters of life.

In fact, anyone who eats much of food without time management considered as a fool. Such a person or people are not wise and cannot be used industrially. And again those people cannot be used by God for His work or any purpose which fits God's people.

Too much of eating can damage your spiritual growth and dismantle your ability and knowledge. It is possible for such people to die suddenly.

These people easily get the spirit of covetousness and they are greedy by nature. Eating of food is good and it is life for human beings, but fasting is better than a bad habit of eating or abusive of food eating.

You need to mind your habit of eating food and measure your volume of intake. Why die before your time? In fact, it will be a grave mistake to let someone who loves food than work to be elected as a leader of a nation.

So, every nation must take a second look when electing a leader for their country. Seriously, what I am saying about food eating should not be taken for granted.

We must take note that those people who love food than work must be avoiding from any activities. There are a lot of imprecations concerning eating and drinking; more seriously the wrong habit of eating. Why these comments?

In fact, eating and drinking is the original source of temptation. It is the channel that the devil always wants to use to destroy the spirit and the body of a man.

We must keep in mind that the devil always wants to use food to tempt us, as he did to our first parents. Man must eat and survive but cannot live alone with bread and survive.

It is our duty and responsibility to work and to eat. This is basic continues life channel for man to sustain his being. But if a man disregards the principle of eating he can lose his life without a savior. Many have failed because of the wrong habit of eating.

Others have died because of the type of food they intending to eat. In fact, the wrong habit of eating can lead us to unforgiving sin. Our nature today is subjected to sin and its practice.

We are at fault and wrongdoings, and our attitude toward food is about 90 percent than other material things we look for. As human beings, we need to be careful about how we seek for food.

Israel's sin against God through what they requested to be eating and many of them died because of the wrong habit of eating. Food should not be our first priority for surviving, but we must note that is part of surviving but not live alone with it.

We need to be temperate in all things, but we must be extra careful about the kind of food we choose to eat. Let's see from the bible what actually happened concerning eating?

Numbers 11:4-6, 33-35

Now the rabble that was among them had a strong craving. And the people of Israel also wept again and said, "Oh that we had meat to eat! We remember the fish we ate in Egypt that cost nothing, the cucumbers, the melons, the leeks, the onions, and the garlic.

But now our strength is dried up, and there is nothing at all but this manna to look at. "While the meat was yet between their teeth, before it was consumed, the anger of the Lord was kindled against the people, and the Lord struck down the people with a very great plague.

Therefore the name of that place was called Kibroth-hattaavah, because there they buried the people who had the craving. From Kibroth-hattaavah the people journeyed to Hazeroth, and they remained at Hazeroth. As human beings, we may eat but we need to be careful about how we crave for.

The devil deceived the first parents to desire and craves for what they have been forbidden to eat. He tempted Jesus (Our Lord) to turn stone to food when He became hungry from fasting. We should not allow eating to occupy our minds or let life be as food-seeking.

It seems others work for food but not life and others too seek to eat but not to survive. What did Jesus said to the devil? ("It is written," 'Man shall not live by bread alone, but by every word that comes from the mouth of God.'") Matthew 4:4

We are not created to survive only by bread alone, but every word that comes from God's mouth. So, our life is not depending on food to endure but on what God word is saying.

This book title is drawing our attention towards what it must be our concern for our daily living more than cloth; shelter, food and so on.

Our duty is to live as heaven think, and not for food and drinking alone. We need to know the negative effect that food can cause our life, and to know the importance of eating well;

simple, best and clean foods for surviving. The Lord has made everything for its purpose, even the wicked for the day of trouble. Let's consider our life and consider eating.

4. Dressing

The second self of human beings identity is dressing code and it is the character of his or her being. God created man in His image and likeness and the man was cloth with the glory and the covering of God.

Our appearance as a human being from the beginning of creation though naked but covered with the glory of God. It was a sin committed that brought the totality of man nakedness.

Human being became naked because of sin. Here the garment of a man was wiped away through sin. Means a man lost his identity as a being. In fact, every character can be identifying by dressing and appearance.

A character cannot be identifying without behaviour and dressing. Our attitude and actions are stands on the dressing code we wear. Maybe one will say dressing cannot identify the person's character or the character has nothing to do with dressing.

But I ask how can you identify a person you did not know or how can you find out the person you are going to meet for the first time amongst the company of a people? Here the person cannot describe his or herself without the cloth which that person wears.

Any kind of clothing of which any person wears is his or her character. Your appearance makes your identity and your dressing proves your thought. Any appearance what so ever maybe signifies light or darkness at that moment the person wears.

Light proves light and darkness proves darkness. You cannot deceive anyone by your sweet words, your dress will prove the kind of person you are. There are many sin waves across the globe but the stronger waves that destroy the spirit, the mind and the body is a wave of bad clothing.

The wider sea and the greatest waves in humans life today is the wave of clothing. Now the most influence and the sin captive tool is the fashion of the day.

Bad clothing destroys the correct mind and good thoughts and it also does away knowledge and wisdom of a person.

The correct and accurate mind can identify by good, simple and nice clothing that someone is wearing. There are no two ways about it, when the person is clothing badly, it proves his or her wrong motive behind that cloth.

We cannot deceive others and ourselves that it is not intentional by wearing bad cloth. We must know that any type or kind of dressing has the purpose by which it was wear.

The doom of the world today is kinds of a dressing moving around. Women of the day are polluting the world by their style of dressing they engage themselves in.

They have become stumble blocks of the day polluting the mind and good thoughts by their style of dressing. This is grievous evil which they are engaging themselves in. Any kind of appearance or wearing of cloth indicates the light or darkness, and as Christians, we need to be careful about the kind of clothes we are engaging ourselves in.

In fact, life is all about character and the knowledge to differentiate right from wrong. But the worst life is to appear wrongly in the manner of your dressing.

The character that was lost in Eden has been restored by Christ death, and it is our duty to go for that lost character. Every child of God is identifying by in and out of appearance reveal.

Means every child of God must appear with purity and good thought through the manifestation of their dress. Here you cannot wear any kind of dress to represent God child.

We need to take note or aware of any kind of dress we are engaging ourselves in. Heaven is watching and weighing those who are faithful to their master any kind of moves.

We are in the end-time history of the world today and all winds across are pointing to one who holds the reward to appear. Never put me wrong or say it is done on what I am commenting about clothing.

Today no one will come out naked when going out from home. Unless the person is mad or mentally challenged, but when someone wears bad or indecent cloth that means the person is mad or mentally challenged.

If not, what the person wants to be or mean? Here any kind of cloth wear has the purpose and meaning or represent of duty or character we must know and understand. Our languages and cultures have a lot to teach and prove the kinds of clothes and their representation.

Every kind of cloth wear must prove identity. Why because the kings of this world have their clothes for their activities which point their state as kings. Soldiers have their clothes for their activities which identify them as soldiers, and the other companies have their logos and other identities.

All these signify the conduct and the manner of their character. The same as God children to prove their character through the kind of dress they wear.

Here God's children need to be brand by their style of dressing. If you dress anyhow, you act anyhow and you act any how; you sin without notification.

Means you reach a point of no sorry and you become dead in sin. Everyone in this world must take this content into consideration that whatever cloth you wear proves your character.

Women of the world today must take this serious without a joke and they should note that dressing kills the mind and good thought which can develop the world more than what we see today.

Heaven is watching; let us appear in the manner of promoting a good atmosphere through modest, decent and beautiful lifestyle clothing. We need to do away pompous kind of dressings that calls attention for no improvement.

And then maintain our dignity as God's children and do all things for the glory of God. Know that your character is your dressing and your dressing is your character and identity.

The bible makes it clear that clothes represent character and good deeds. Let's consider this quotes; in Revelation 19:7, 8

Says: Let us rejoice and exult

and give him the glory,

for the marriage of the Lamb has come,

and his Bride has made herself ready;

it was granted her to clothe herself

with fine linen, bright and pure"—

for the fine linen is the righteous deeds of the saints

This bible verse is letting us wear the bright and pure garment, which means we must live with good conscientiousness and in behaviour.

That is, our appearance must have no bad comments and results towards those around us.

Another scripture says; likewise, also that women should adorn themselves in respectable apparel, with modesty and self-control, not with braided hair and gold or pearls or costly attire, but with what is proper for women who profess godliness—with good works. Let a woman learn quietly with all submissiveness. (Timothy 2:9-11)

What we must know and notice is that any bad appearance blocks the idea of communication between two parties or person and it destroys the knowledge and wisdom that needs to apply for human development. And it is shameful and abhorring in human trade to dressing indecent attire.

Here women in the world today must be careful about the way they present themselves concerning their dress. Bad character is like an indecent dress and also bad appearance is like a bad character.

Everyone must know that any appearance that is contrary to acceptable dress is a law-breaking. As heaven-born children we need to make the world good and peaceful through our appearance and in dressing. We should not forget our name and identity. Maybe one will say any dress is a dress and there is no bad attire.

But I will say there is a difference between river and lake, and there is a difference in structure between man and woman. So as to the clothes style meant to wear, and there is a difference between soldier and police but they are all security service personnel.

What do I mean? There must be differences between God children and the children of the world. But this is to appear in the attire and the personality.

In fact, if there is anything that can be used to describe a man, it is his cloth and appearance. And there is no character without action and personality but rest on the clothes wear. We must, therefore, be careful on how we present ourselves. We will appear on a judgment seat and account for our deeds.

5. Walking

Our movement as human beings needs careful consideration. Life development and success depends on our move. The absence of movement makes life unfruitful and burdensome.

The man became complete through movement and action. Without movement, there is no life improvement.

Our movement makes us a living being. All living things move and act. Any mobile or move have the purpose by which it was intended.

God created us as living beings and not as inaction or inactivity beings. But any kind of move or walk defines the thought of that move, whether it is a human being or an animal.

So, walking makes a man a man that is a complete being. Walking speaks more than a mouth. One thing we need to know about walking is a working tool and the development and success key. Any sin that human beings have committed was caused by our walk or movement.

The mind and the leg are co-workers they move together by agreement. Bad motives are bad walks and bad walks are bad motives and acts. Whatever the move or walk makes the mind direction.

It is necessary for us to have knowledge of our movement and the purpose by which we move or walk.

Walking can speak more than the sea waves and can destroy things more than a bomb. Walking is a gift and talent as well and our human achievement is control by walking.

In fact, there can be no progress without movement or walking. What are all these comments? In fact, our nature today is totally sinful and there is nothing good in us.

Walking is a blessing and a development key. But bad walking is a snare that destroys the soul and the spirit; because it reveals the direction of the mind and thought. Any act of movement reveals the character and the motive.

Bad walking reveals bad thought and it better die than to walk wrongly. Walking has a great impression than talking and dancing. Why because every human being walks more than talking.

One thing we need to know and to keep in mind is that our being is all about movement. We need to mind our walk and our act to prevent damage.

Good walking welcomes peace and brings liberty to the soul. Any style of walking determines the person character and prove the motive whether it is good or bad.

This title (Think as you are in Paradise) means be careful about all your movement and thought. In fact, walking can prove the person success or not and it is a life motive for progress or not.

Walking reveals the kind of speech any person have or it is a witness of one's type of speech. Moreover, as the man walks, it is the same as he talks.

Further, the speech of every man is his walk and it is a witnessed of his state or personality. Pride walks are pride talk and bad walks are bad character and thoughts.

When you walk indecent, you speak like arrogant and prove indiscipline acts. We must, therefore, know that whichever walk we display or steps we make speak to others for good or bad results.

Any walk that we intend needs to be measured only for good and not for evil; else it will lead us into destruction.

Everyone needs to train his or her self-concerning the steps we make and practice a decent walk for good name. Angels of heaven are taking notes on every step we make and record every motive behind.

As human beings, our names go with a walk and talk, whether it is good or bad makes a name or character in heaven.

Here the only identity that makes a stranger description concerning someone character or nature; when the person is silent or out of speech is walking.

Walking is the act of conversation which proves the person's character or behaviour for good or evil to those around.

There are many noises all over the globe but walking talks more than the noise. You will never be agreeing with me but it is true.

The only sign that one can notice from the other is his or her walk. Else you cannot identify anyone concerning his or her character unless the person speaks.

We are in the world that is full of sins and disorder but everyone needs to be careful concerning the walking.

We are in the end history of this world; the waves testify that something is coming. Everyone needs to be careful and do things right.

There is no excuse concerning our deeds. We must keep our steps well and measure each walk we make.

Let us put away stubbornness walk and then manage the walk for the talk to prevent accident for ourselves and others. Let's take note from this scripture;

The Lord said: Because the daughters of Zion are haughty
and walk with outstretched necks,
glancing wantonly with their eyes,
mincing along as they go,
tinkling with their feet,
therefore the Lord will strike with a scab
the heads of the daughters of Zion,
and the Lord will lay bare their secret parts. (Isaiah 3:16, 17)

We must watch out concerning proper life matters and then leave correct history for our children who are not yet born. Life is good.

6. Looking

Looking makes a man up to the point and makes the movement easy and meaningful. The light of a man is his eye and the whole being.

When you close your eyes, you cannot move well as you want it. In order to discover something good for life, you need to observe in order to bring out the successful answer.

Eyeing is important and good for the brain to distinguish right from the wrong. But bad looking destroys the whole being and makes the wrong direction for the soul.

Our life cannot be complete without eyeing. The light of a man is his eye and the human movements depend on the eye to find way in and out.

Our existence as human being completely depends on the eye for act and doings. In fact, there can be no development without an eye. Here our eye is our being.

One thing we need to know is that knowledge gain comes from eyeing or looking. Our mind or brain response whether good or bad depends on eyeing.

When the eye is good, the whole being will be good, and again when the eye is bad the being will be bad.

Our nature cannot perform well without an eye. Everyone needs to be very careful when eyeing something. Bad looking destroys good thought and damage the brain for correct responses.

As human beings, we cherish by looking and perform through the act of eyeing. To love and convert stands on looking. Any act or performance comes by looking.

Eyeing is the most necessary gift in humans' life and it is the highest gift or tool for activities. In fact, it is a basic discovery tool for acquiring knowledge.

But one thing we need to know is that our knowledge can destroy through bad looking. In fact, the world has been ready damaged by sin and the sin was first generated by looking. Let's take note of this scripture: Genesis 3:6, 7

Says:

So when the woman saw that the tree was good for food, and that it was a delight to the eyes, and that the tree was to be desired to make one wise, she took of its fruit and ate, and she also gave some to her husband who was with her, and he ate.

Then the eyes of both were opened, and they knew that they were naked. And they sewed fig leaves together and made themselves loincloths. Looking is an act of assessing something or taking note of things through observation.

Any knowledge that we intend to gain comes by eyeing. In fact, today the nature of man as a sinful being was first cause by eyeing. Looking generates kinds of thought but the results justify by thought invented.

As human beings, we need to be very careful about how we eye or thought or observe of things.

In Mathew 5:27-30 says;

"You have heard that it was said, you shall not commit adultery.' But I say to you that everyone who looks at a woman with lustful intent has already committed adultery with her in his heart.

If your right eye causes you to sin, tear it out and throw it away. For it is better that you lose one of your members than that your whole body is thrown into hell. And if your right-hand causes you to sin, cut it off and throw it away.

For it is better that you lose one of your members than that your whole body goes into hell. Here it is better to lose your one eye than to take the whole being to the hell.

This is serious saying by Jesus. Our eyes can cause us much trouble and damage the whole being. Eyeing is good but bad looking cause death instead of life and knowledge.

We must keep mind that every bad look kill the correct thought and injuries the personality. We need to be careful on the way we look at things and take good thought to prevent the soul from damage.

We need also to know that our thoughts are our looks and our looks are our thoughts. Everyone must be considerate in looking and in thoughts. We will be accountable for every look and thought we invented.

As human beings, our life must be in the manner of modest and to avoid damage. We need to have a positive mind and thought in the way we look at things. We need to take good thought and observe things carefully.

Our eyes make life better and profitable but bad or lustful eyes destroy development and the soul. Let's consider this scripture:

1stPeter 5:8, 9

Be sober-minded; be watchful. Your adversary the devil prowls around like a roaring lion, seeking someone to devour. Resist him, firm in your faith, knowing that the same kinds of suffering are being experienced by your brotherhood throughout the world.

In order for the mind to have a good thought or concentration sometimes stands on the things we always watch or look.

The mind sometimes generates a lot of thought by an excess watch or continues attention.

Think as you are in Heaven or Paradise as this book title is reminding us to God and then living according to the principles of heaven on this earth.

7. Dancing

Dancing is good and it brings joy; health and healing to the body. Dancing and health are brothers and opens the mind and make it active. To dance is to be happy and to be happy is to dance.

Dancing comes by exciting and joy or when you hear good news. It is part of our nature for entertainment and it is also a gift.

When you dance, you progress and reduce stress. Dancing is the art of communication and happiness. Any art of entertainment that exempts dancing is the out of joy. And there can be no dancing without happiness.

So, dance comes by cheerfulness and it is a sign of positive results. Dancing raises high motives and bring correct thought.

But there are two types of dancing, one for a bad habit to improve sexual excitement and the other for fun and happiness. The most sinful tool that calls for sexual intercourse is bad dancing and the most disgraceful art in the world is bad dancing.

In fact, in the history of this world concerning art and skills or gifts that easily generates bad thought is through indecent dance. Any kind of dance can influence for good or bad results.

The art of dancing is the art of exercising the body for a good atmosphere. Good dancing is health sources for the brain and the whole body, and it is the art of rejoicing.

It improves the bones for strength and revives the spirit. We need to dance when we are happy but we must take care of the dance we exhibit.

Bad dancing can cause a lot of damages to the brain and can stop the brain from good thinking. Bad dancing can generate lust and dismantle the brain from good judgment at the moment it displays.

But good dance is a great activity to pursue at almost any age provided you are in; it is proper health to continue in regular **dancing** for life.

So, dancing is more than the exploring of different ways to make a shape or learning a series of steps to music; it is a way of moving the body as an instrument of expression and communication.

There are different kinds of dancing but it has two categories of influence. It is whether for good, fitness and the positive result for brain or bad, fitness and negative result for the brain.

Why am I saying these comments? In fact, it is better to exercise for fitness than to dance badly for fitness.

It can kill your good thought and the correct inner joy or happiness of your being. It can also have a bad influence on those around you and kills the beauty of the being.

Dancing is everywhere in the world and it is a gift that generates happiness. We all need to know that, bad dancing is poison for the brain and the killer of a good habit.

Why because the motive behind such dance promotes lust and sexual invention through the act and kind of drive. There are kinds of behaviours or conduct reveal in dancing and every conduct or act revealed has the result of a positive and negative effect.

These acts or conduct that reveals cause death or life for someone. All that I want to say is that; we need to be very careful when we are happy or dancing through happiness.

Dancing is not bad but it is bad when we over dance or abusive the dancing. It is good for everyone to dancing when you are happy, but be careful not to dance above the good charisma in the dance.

We need to be careful on this earth because our creator is in front, back and above considering our move and conducts towards Him and others.

We will one day going to account for every deed we exhibited. Let's take note of these scriptures: Eccl. 12:13, 14, Micah 6:8 The end of the matter; all has been heard.

Fear God and keep his commandments, for this is the whole duty of man. For God will bring every deed into judgment, with every secret thing, whether good or evil.

He has told you, O man, what is good;
and what does the Lord require of you
but to do justice, and to love kindness,
and to walk humbly with your God?

As human beings, we should not forget ourselves but we need to remember our creator and behaviour as His law requires. Think as you are in Paradise.

Means be careful and behave well in all your doings and be sensible of your actions concerning anything you intend to do. Be a blessing to all who come to you and then make your life dear!

8. Sleeping

The peak of healthful living practice that makes our health well balance is sleeping.

The body repairs all the broken cells in the time of resting at night. Rest makes the body regain its strength and then set it for other activities.

Everyone needs sufficient rest or sleep at night to preserve his or her fitness balance. The body needs to rest at night. We should avoid working at night if it is possible.

If not, let everyone have some time to rest or sleep to regain the sufficient strength that the body needs. Without rest or correct sleep, the mind or brain will fail on it balancing activity.

Or it cannot work correctly as it should. Sleepless night makes imbalance thought and then worsen the eye of the brain.

That is, it reduces the strength and the ability of the brain. So, sufficient sleep is the balm for the brain that makes it work correctly.

It opens the eye of the brain to see properly and then boost the understanding. When you avoid sleep at the night, you avoid the correct physical balance of your health for the day activity.

You should not joke on your health for the sake of making money at any time without rest. Else, you will reduce your life span. Have you ask yourself about why God divided the day with darkness and light?

It is a balance move with equal hours. Sometimes the light part of the day, takes some long hours than the night hours. So to the night hours makes the same.

It shows the beauty of creation movement. This shows the emergency at work in our daily life of which maybe the style of living can be change for a setting reason.

Yet, it should not be a continuous habit to do away proper health principles. To think of good health, there must be a proper sleep habit of each human being. When you do away proper sleep, you do away correct working hours and proper wellbeing.

That is, you cannot work comfortably as you should. This does not do away hard working principle. However, care must be taking. Then again never take the light day activities into sleeping hours.

Else, poverty will knock your door. Make use of the light day to have sufficient means for the future to prevent wreck at your old age.

Do not over sleep but try to prevent laziness with adequate sleeping which boost the health of the being. Those who want to take the whole hours to work will be shortening their days of life. Let there be a balance in everything we do.

Everyone needs a meaningful sleep habit to restore both mental and spiritual balance growth. The natural practice in everything we do makes it well balance and then brings successful fruit.

Let no one abuse the natural practice instituted by God for our wellbeing. We must avoid man made practice of eating and sleeping behavior to prevent severe headaches and fatal death.

Sleeping is the natural tonic for the brain function which built the positive thoughts for creations of the light days' work. Naturally, our whole being begins proper functioning after correct sleep or some rest of the day.

When the brain comes out from the days stress, it brings atmosphere of peace and comfort for the whole being.

A reasonable thing comes by reasonable thoughts, and then reasonable thought brings positive results.

When the mind is free from stress, it resulted joy for the whole being and then work well for profitable results. So sleep is the natural remedy for the brain and the body to function accordingly.

Let no one joke about his or her health, because the whole wealth of the world depends on the ability of the health that the world holds.

The amount of work done on every day depends on the amount of health we have. The amount of wealth of the day resulted by the amount of health we proceed. So, health is all about everything that goes on day.

Without proper health, there will be no fruit of the day. Let us consider our ways and doings then to protect our health matters to fulfill our missions on the day.

It is appointed for us to do the Masters work, because there is coming bad days which no one can work. Your health is your wealth and your wealth is your reward that makes you a successful being.

Let everyone try to prevent diseases by living according to the natural laws and health principles. Life is all about health and the rest is the addition which fulfills our joy and peace.

My brethren, I pray for you in all matters of life that it shall be well with you and then have good health. Let us consider our sleep when the time is due and then to avoid stressful thoughts to have sound sleep to prevent brain tumor and other diseases.

Let us prevent bad and other stressful matters that abuse the brain from functioning properly and then keep ourselves from unnecessary thoughts.

In everything, let us give thanks to the Lord and then leave stressful matters to Him. Let us leave everything to God, for the days trouble is heavy and bad upon it.

To God everything is possible and He knows our troubles and problems. He is ready to help, because He cares for us. Let us leave everything to Him and then have our peace to fulfill our sound sleep every night.

Sufficient sleep that someone's have in a day; prolongs his or her days and then add wealth and health for the waste days ahead.

The system strength concerning every human being depends on the amount of peace it has. For us to work with enthusiasm, it depends on the amount of joy that the brain has from the stressful matters.

Rest when you are tired but work according to your ability to protect your wealth and health. Try to avoid stressful issues and then have rest for your soul.

9. Your talent

Our system has been programming with all the necessary things we need for the life journey. The world and everything in them is in raw state. That is, in fresh or original to make use for other things.

Let us learn more about this raw state issue that God intentionally did it. God want us to learn more and develop well.

In fact, when it comes to creation, there is no limit in anything, yet death has deformed the continuation of human development.

Why creatures in it raw state? What is the purpose? Work is the formation of life and the meaning of surviving. When there is no work, the object of life is lost and human beings will be useless of been created by God!

So God created man to be useful and makes life through activities. The whole system of life is been industrious; else the life will be meaningless.

When we talk of life, we talk of activities or work. So, when there is no work, there is no life and creation of this world will be out of meaning.

God is God of activities and that makes Him God! Human beings are not created to be lazy or idle.

So, the creation of this world became meaningful when the man was created to till and to keep the land. For us to be useful, God filled this world with raw materials for us to use them for activities that suit the meaning of life for our benefits.

So, life is work and work is life and that makes us meaningful human beings. We were created for work or activities and that makes meaningful beings.

Human development became meaningful through these raw materials making use of them. In all, the working materials were created before man for him to have meaningful life by making use of them.

The creation consists of so many fields of knowledge and materials useful for our development.

For us to make proper use of them, talents were given to each individual. Meaningful life consists of abilities or skills for development. So, each one of us has the skill by which he or she can live with.

Your talent makes your condition of life through its application. It is your life and functioning as being. When you fail to use your talent or ability, you fail to function as human being.

Your health is your second self of your talent, when you abuse your health, you abuse your talent.

It is the same as you fail to use your talent. God gave us ability by which we can live with. That is, each one of us has a gift to live with for development.

We were created for activities and purpose. It is our wealth that promotes the life we have. We need to use our gifts to promote our life.

Do not put aside your talent of which your growth depend on. Never abuse it through inactivity.

Yet, make use of it to improve your life and your wealth. It is your health, your joy and your keys that open your success.

You need to regard it whether big or small. It is a tool by which your life success depends on. If you put aside your talent, you put aside your destiny.

It is your joy and health that prolongs your life span. Everyone needs to use his or her talent then to make a reasonable life. The world needs to benefit from yours.

Do not become useless by putting aside your talent of which your life development stand on. You need to make use of your talent to improve your working ability for successful life.

It is your means for development that improve your health and wealth. Do not joke of it, yet try and use them, whether you have one or more. If you don't use your talent, then you don't want to have a better life.

The servant who is useless must be cast out into deep darkness that belongs to the wicked. Those lazy people will have their part in everlasting sorrow.

If you consider your gift and then make use of it, you consider your wealth and health as well. Let everyone use his or her talent to prevent poverty and sorrowful life. Your gift or faculty is your means for life improvement.

Build your faculties through activities to fulfill your goal of which you were created for. Let the world recognize you through your ability, you will be bless and become blessing for others.

Let us develop together by making use of our talents to improve ourselves and the world we live.

Do not be a slothful servant, yet let the Master applauds you for making use of that gift given to you. Do not be a dead person through inactivity. Wake up and use your natural gift.

10. Your Soul diet

As human beings, we were created with dust and the spirit which is the breath of God. We became living beings through breath or the spirit of God.

As the body needs food to grow, so the spirit also needs food to grow as well. We are two fold elements that make us living beings. Our bodies build and grow by the food we eat.

As the body needs to grow, so the spirit needs grow. What is the diet of the spirit or the soul? What makes the spirit weak? What affect the spirit health? Is there anything that can clammy our spirit growth?

What is the soul food? What must we do to revive our spirit as individual? What must we avoid to make our spirit feels better?

Our physical nature needs to be built and nourish well. Again the spiritual nature also needs to be built and nourish well.

Both needs better health to make us strong in doing all things. When one is weak, the other does not function well.

As the body laughs when it get food, so is the spirit laugh when it get food. We always feed the body more than the spirit.

It must be equal sharing, not one should suffer hunger and the other enjoy. So, what is the food for our soul or the spirit?

First all, is the word of God; proper Psalms or hymns or songs, correct happiness, act of kindness, act of honesty, act of faith, act of correct love, forceful act and prayers.

These are the foods that sustain the spirit of our being. It is the fruit that nourish the spirit of our being. A man became a living soul through the body and the spirit together, which is the breath of God.

When one is absent, the other cannot be functioning. We should equally feed the soul as we feed the body. This makes our health complete and balance.

When the body is feed, the spirit also must be feed at the same time. Our health cannot be complete, when we close our eyes on spiritual matters or do away the necessary things concerning our spiritual being.

Our health must be equally build on both wings. That makes us physically and spiritually sound and strong.

Fasting and prayers are the special for food for the spirit, and that builds the inner being for correct communication to God. It brings the beauty of the spirit and then magnify it strength.

Correct Bible studies cleansing the inner being and brings spiritual growth and energy. Intentionally sin deforms our spirit and then deteriorates the whole ability of the soul.

The accurate health of our being is to balance the physical and the spiritual living for both needed diet.

It is not all meat that we should consume, yet we must consume the recommended ones according to the Bible and health principles.

Some food intake can damage your spirit and body without repairs. As human beings, we need to respect our creator and then keep His words concerning our diet.

Let all keep watching and then take notes of our diet; and then prolong our vanity days to fulfill everlasting one with vigilance. You must mind your diet and then mind your future. If you reject to take note of your diet, then you refuse to fulfill your destiny.

Notes of Life:

Circumstances are the guides of life which awaking the person or the soul from been wreck by the world matters that fails better life.

It is better for everyone to face some challenge in life; else the person will not learn anything or will fail of proper management.

It opens our eyes and then builds us for good standing. Life is not like running water which goes smooth. It must face some challenges for it to be better live.

Everyone must note that, without challenge or trials, the life cannot be properly managed. All things work together for our good by the purpose of God.

We are in the world of troubles which needs daily guides and proper management. There are lots which we must learn and then take note off. Every day brings new things and then leaves us history which can be learned later by our children who are not yet born.

We need to fight day and night to make the life on it way. No one knows which hour or day will be a bad storm. We all need to prepare and then wait and watch.

The world is running out, things are not as it was at the beginning. There are so many changes and things are deteriorating day and night. There are many cries going on, fears of wants have covered many peoples mind.

It is because so many people love the world and its goods. There must be circumstances that can alert us from slumber. So, circumstance build and bring us back on track.

Our situation as human beings lack responding to righteousness of life. As it is, there is no way that Ethiopian can change his or her burn body. This is our situation as human beings; there is no way that we can change our sinful heart.

We need God intervention to have this change of heart. Concerning this state of ourselves, it is difficult for us to do well or respond to God law which maintains proper life.

So, He (God) permits trials on our ways for us to remember Him in these times of troubles. Then to seek help from Him and to move, else, no one will recognition of Him.

This is our condition when sin comes in our ways. The children Israel desert walk is the best example for us to know the disciplines of God.

As we journey towards the Promised Land, we will face many troubles in our ways. It is not to discourage us, yet to make us strong and then to take care.

Our way of life in this earth is very tragedy. Everyone wants to live by his or her wishes. Many people love the world and its matters. The Christians journey to the Heaven is not the matters of world and its agreements.

Yet, it is a reasonable service and renew of mind for proper human aid and good works. In order for us not go astray from the right path, then comes in circumstance to aid us from straying.

Trials are proper life aid that put us on track and then make us strong as Christians. It opens our eyes and then prompts us to seek God. It awaking us from sleeps and then makes us examining our ways of life.

It is God wish for us to have eternal life. That is why He permits those trials to keep us on track. God does not hesitate on His promise as some thinks.

Yet He has patience for us to come to repentance and does not want us to perish, but to have everlasting life.

This is the way sometimes God lead us to be alert and be strong of our daily life. The lessons of life are the teachers teaching us to take care in our entire move. We are to be strong and enthusiast in all our doings.

So, trials are key guides, which awake us from deviating. The journey of the children of Israel in the wilderness is an example for us as Christians today in our daily life.

The matters we come across at in our daily life are the lessons of our journey towards the promise land.

Our daily life must come out with good report and records, which will be a witness for our position each one deserve.

We should not worry about the hardship that comes in but we must focus on the reward or the price. Trials are the efficacies that maintain the better growth of Christian's life standard demand wishes.

So, it is not God intention to kill or makes us worried in our daily life, but to help us fit into our position which He has setup. The circumstance that comes into our way is the benefit of our life journey that suits the call. Let us consider our doings and change our way of life.

11. Your Harvest

How do you respect the time and its movement in this life? How do you manage your time? Your respect for time reflects the situation you are in now.

Your time will never change the condition of your situation unless you respect it as you move forward. So respect time whilst you have life. Note that time is life.

So many people in this world have become poor because they have little or no regard for the time given to them by God.

You will be victorious by keeping your time in every situation. Nobody knows what will be the condition the next time. So be prepared at each time and each moment.

Your time conditions are the situations you are in. That is, the reward of your time predicts its condition. Your condition today shows what you did yesterday. And that is your reward for the day. Respect time as you move on in this world. Your condition today is the result and the fruitage of what you did yesterday.

Every life starts from a point and that point is the beginning of the life race. Your life records depend on your actions and behavior. Every action of your life determines your success and defeat.

Every act of your life has fruits to bear, and these fruits bring your destiny. Destiny brings your real character, and that is the result of your life.

Whatever you do impact your life. You cannot hide anything in this world and still walk freely. The rotation of life will ensure you get back to your threshold.

Do right and you will harvest right. You can never cheat anyone; time will tell. As the world or earth rotates, so also the life you are living. Watch out! Every action returns to the actor, and the result is the reward to the one who acted.

12. Take care

Your thoughts are your actions, and your actions are your thoughts. Also, your thought gives identification to the eye in all situations – whether good or bad – and gives signals to the whole face.

Bad thoughts can damage your life, stop your inner joy and demolish your real understanding. Your movement in life, sometimes, shows your thought at that moment.

Your fears, your joy, your boldness, your willingness, and your competency stand on your thought.

You will not be well developed unless you have the right thought. What you think about determines how you behave.

Your thoughts influence your speech, and your language gives an identity to you as a person. Your speech shows your thought. If your thought is right, your action will be right. The bad speech shows your thought.

Actions are the result of your thought. Good behavior is fruit of right thought. Right thought brings peace, good health, and happiness to you.

Your progress depends on the right thought. Your thought defines your personality, and that determines your stature as a human being.

Whatever you do – whether good or bad – depends on thought. Your good works are your thought, and your bad works too are your thought.

Your thought will determine your life span, and your life span is the result of your thought. This result could be a healthy or weak body.

That is, your state as human being rests on your positive thought, which makes you a real human.

Your sorrows depend on your thought; so does your happiness. Being sorrowful or happy depends on your thought. Watch what you think, for it determines your state as a human being. Think well. Your desire for right thought will let you think well.

13. Becoming Your Faith

Attitude is your reaction towards everything you do or your willingness to act. Your state today is the result of your attitude yesterday.

Your faith becomes your life and everything concerning your feeling. Faith is about life and how you move and the attitude you show.

You are your faith. That is, your knowledge and understanding about your move. Your reactions identify your belief. You become your faith through your act or attitude.

How heavy is your faith? What do you believe? Your faith determines your weight, and your weight determines your success.

Your attitude is the key that to opens your success. How do you welcome people? How do you welcome your work? What is your goal?

How do you do your things? How do you feel when it comes to working? What is your faith? How do you feel? You are who you are because of your faith.

Your faith is your attitude and your words. What is your response when you heard something? How do you behave toward circumstances? When the faith is big, it shows the amount of work that can be done.

What are your reactions towards work? How interested are you when it comes to working? Your response to work informs the amount of your wealth. Your willingness determines your state.

Attitude brings about the wellbeing of every situation of your life. Behavior is a product of an attitude, and your actions are results of attitude.

Life cannot be whole without a good attitude. By considering your attitude will lead you to a good position, in order to please God.

So many people in this world have become miserable because of their attitude. Your feelings are not always right but your feelings can bring you up or down, and this is influenced by your attitude.

Your attitude can make you benefit; it could also land you into trouble. Your situation is your attitude page, and that page is your reward.

You become what you believe and then make your destiny. Your reward will determine your faith and that is you today. It is for good or bad? It can change for the best, if you believe.

For Good Living and Knowledge Gain!
B. B. S. LIFE BOOKS.

You Are Your Thoughts Page

Also by Bernard Benson Sarfo

The Fact Among Facts (1st)
The Fact Among Facts

Standalone
The Youth Murderer
Be Original Not a Copy
The Christians Science or Scholarship
Precious than Paradise
Habit Makes Future
A shelter from storm and rain
The Science of Life
The Strongest Lion Knockback
The Perfect and Inspiring City
Above Hope, Faith and Love
The Hero's Brave Decisions
The Weakest Among Plants
The Hero's Brave Decisions
Doing Above The Ability
The Wisdom Beyond Power And Greatness

Heavier Than the Heavens
The Academics Brains and Recreation Logics
The Strange Voice
The Chaotic World
Don't Miss Your Flight
Let the Nations Ponder
You Are Your Thoughts

About the Author

Bernard Benson Sarfo is an acquainted architectural designer and a motivational speaker.He is a gifted teacher who continues to motivate and encourage many.

Read more at https://www.amazon.com//author/bbslifebooks.